The Missing Voices in EdTech

CORWIN CONNECTED EDUCATORS SERIES

Content Curation: How to Avoid Information Overload
By Steven W. Anderson @web20classroom

5 Skills for the Global Learner: What Everyone Needs to Navigate the Digital World
By Mark Barnes @markbarnes19

Teaching the iStudent: A Quick Guide to Using Mobile Devices and Social Media in the K-12 Classroom
By Mark Barnes @markbarnes19

Connected Leadership: It's Just a Click Away
By Spike Cook @DrSpikeCook

All Hands on Deck: Tools for Connecting Educators, Parents, and Communities
By Brad Currie @bradmcurrie

The Missing Voices in EdTech: Bringing Diversity Into EdTech
By Rafranz Davis @RafranzDavis

Flipping Leadership Doesn't Mean Reinventing the Wheel
By Peter DeWitt @PeterMDeWitt

The Edcamp Model: Powering Up Professional Learning
By the Edcamp Foundation @EdcampUSA

Worlds of Making: Best Practices for Establishing a Makerspace for Your School
By Laura Fleming @NMHS_lms

Leading Professional Learning: Tools to Connect and Empower Teachers
By Tom Murray @thomascmurray and Jeff Zoul @Jeff_Zoul

Empowered Schools, Empowered Students: Creating Connected and Invested Learners
By Pernille Ripp @pernilleripp

Blogging for Educators: Writing for Professional Learning
By Starr Sackstein @mssackstein

Principal Professional Development: Leading Learning in the Digital Age
By Joseph Sanfelippo @Joesanfelippofc and Tony Sinanis @TonySinanis

The Power of Branding: Telling Your School's Story
By Tony Sinanis @TonySinanis and Joseph Sanfelippo @Joesanfelippofc

The Relevant Educator: How Connectedness Empowers Learning
By Tom Whitby @tomwhitby and Steven W. Anderson @web20classroom

The Missing Voices in EdTech

Bringing Diversity Into EdTech

Rafranz Davis

CORWIN
A SAGE Company

CORWIN
A SAGE Company

FOR INFORMATION:

Corwin
A SAGE Company
2455 Teller Road
Thousand Oaks, California 91320
(800) 233-9936
www.corwin.com

SAGE Publications Ltd.
1 Oliver's Yard
55 City Road
London EC1Y 1SP
United Kingdom

SAGE Publications India Pvt. Ltd.
B 1/I 1 Mohan Cooperative Industrial Area
Mathura Road, New Delhi 110 044
India

SAGE Publications Asia-Pacific Pte. Ltd.
3 Church Street
#10-04 Samsung Hub
Singapore 049483

Copyright © 2015 by Corwin

Printed in the United States of America

A catalog record of this book is available from the Library of Congress.

ISBN 978-1-4833-7187-0

This book is printed on acid-free paper.

Executive Editor: Arnis Burvikovs
Associate Editor: Ariel Price
Editorial Assistant: Andrew Olson
Production Editor: Amy Schroller
Copy Editor: Pam Schroeder
Typesetter: C&M Digitals (P) Ltd.
Proofreader: Penelope Sippel
Cover and Interior Design: Janet Kiesel
Marketing Manager: Lisa Lysne

Certified Chain of Custody
SUSTAINABLE FORESTRY INITIATIVE
Promoting Sustainable Forestry
www.sfiprogram.org
SFI-01268

SFI label applies to text stock

15 16 17 18 19 10 9 8 7 6 5 4 3 2 1

Contents

Preface ix

About the Author xi

Introduction 1

1. Understanding Diversity 3

    Confronting My Thinking on Diversity 3

    Defining Diverse Voices 4

        Why Diversity Matters 4

        Chapter 1 Reflections 5

2. Teacher Voice in EdTech 7

    Vignette: The Voice of the Teacher Is Critical 8

    Barriers to Teacher Voice 9

    Teachers' Perceptions of Technology 9

        Teacher Tech Type Reflections 11

    Campus Leaders: Developing Teacher Tech Leaders 11

        Ideas for Developing Teacher Tech Leaders

           on Campus 12

    Teacher Voice in Technology Professional

        Development 13

        Chapter 2 Reflections 16

3. The Student Learner Perspective 17

    Vignette: I Want to Use My Technology 17

    Students Have Ideas Too 19

        Student Ideas for Mobile Devices 19

Student Voice and EdTech   20

Three Simple Solutions for Engaging Student Voice   21

The Missing Voice of Students of Poverty   22

Vignette: I Didn't Have a Choice but to Work
Night Shift   23

Technology for Students With No Choice   24

Chapter 3 Reflections   25

4. Beyond Pencil Skirts and High Heels:
Women of EdTech   27

Vignette: I Started With a Why . . . I Continue
for the Who   27

Connected Women as Serious Voices of
Tech Influence   31

Empowering EdTech Women Leaders at School   33

Chapter 4 Reflections   35

5. The Unspoken Inequity: People of Color in EdTech   37

Vignette: Connecting in EdTech Beyond Race   37

Recognizing Expertise at the School Level   39

Breaking Cultural Code: Empowering to Share   40

Connecting Teachers of Color   42

Chapter 5 Reflections   45

A Personal Reflection on Missing Voices   47

Additional Resources   49

Preface

Welcome to the Corwin Connected Educators Series.

Last year, Ariel Price, Arnis Burvikovs, and I assembled a great list of authors for the Fall 2014 books in the Corwin Connected Educators Series. As leaders in their field of connected education, they all provided practical, short books that helped educators around the world find new ways to connect. The books in the Spring 2015 season will be equally as beneficial for educators.

We have all seen momentous changes for educators. States debate the use of the Common Core State Standards, and teachers and leaders still question the use of technology, while some of their students have to disconnect and leave it at home because educators do not know how to control learning on devices. Many of the Series authors worked in schools where they were sometimes the only ones trying to encourage use of technology tools at the same time their colleagues tried to ban it. Through their PLNs they were able to find others who were trying to push the envelope.

This spring, we have a list of authors who are known for pushing the envelope. Some are people who wrote books for the Fall 2014 season, while others are brand new to the series. What they have in common is that they see a different type of school for students, and they write about ideas that all schools should be practicing now.

Rafranz Davis discusses *The Missing Voices in EdTech*. She looks at and discusses how we need to bring more diverse voices to the connected world because those voices will enrich how we learn and the way we think. Starr Sackstein, a teacher in New York City writes about blogging for reflection in her book *Blogging for Educators*. Twitter powerhouse Steven W. Anderson returns to the Series to bring us *Content Curation*, as do the very engaging Joseph M. Sanfelippo and Tony Sinanis with their new book, *Principal Professional Development*. Mark Barnes rounds out the comeback authors with his book on *5 Skills for the Global Learner*. Thomas C. Murray and Jeffrey Zoul bring a very practical "how to" for teachers and leaders in their book *Leading Professional Learning* and Makerspaces extraordinaire Laura Fleming brings her expertise with *Worlds of Making*.

I am insanely excited about this book series. As a former principal I know time is in short supply, and teachers and leaders need something they can read today and put into practice tomorrow. That is the exciting piece about technology; it can help enhance your practices by providing you with new ideas and helping you connect with educators around the world.

The books can be read in any order, and each will provide information on the tools that will keep us current in the digital age. We also look forward to continuing the series with more books from experts on connectedness.

As Michael Fullan has been saying for many years, technology is not the right driver, good pedagogy is, and the books in this series focus on practices that will lead to good pedagogy in our digital age. To assist readers in their connected experience, we have created the Corwin Connected Educators companion website where readers can connect with the authors and find resources to help further their experience. The website can be found at www .corwin.com/connectededucators. It is our hope that we can meet you where you are in your digital journey, and bring you up to the next level.

Peter DeWitt, EdD @PeterMDeWitt

About the Author

Rafranz Davis is an instructional technology specialist for a Dallas/Fort Worth area school district. As an advocate for passion-based learning, Rafranz uses her experience as a secondary math educator to help teachers integrate technology using innovative teaching strategies aimed at empowering students to be autonomous learners. As a writer and speaker, Davis frequently draws upon her background as a parent and woman of color to offer ideas and insight into how technology can be used in schools to not only break barriers but to provide opportunities and instruments for diverse learners' voices.

I dedicate this book to my parents, James A. Davis, Jr. and Beverly Davis, for always pushing me to proudly use my own voice.

Introduction

When I was presented with the opportunity to write this book, I hesitated for a second as to whether or not I could in fact write to the needs of this topic. It was important to me that I didn't just write a book that states the obvious but one that would offer schools real solutions. Over the course of the last few months, I embarked upon a collaborative journey of discovery to truly understand the lack of diversity in EdTech. In doing that, I found that many of my initial thoughts were valid, but quite a few of them needed deep thought and review. As a learner, I am most proud of the personal growth that I experienced as a result of this process.

As you read this book, I encourage you to utilize the reflective tools built within each chapter. Have discussions with others. Reflect on your own thinking, and be open to seeing the real issues that we often miss in our schools and in this industry.

Ultimately, my goal is that we can move toward purposeful dialogue and make subtle changes that can impact our schools in great ways. In order to do that, we must adjust our systemic norms to close the informational and instructional gaps created by our long-standing issues with diversity.

While there are countless forms of diversity, this book directly speaks to the missing voices of teachers, students in poverty, women, and people of color in EdTech. In addition, this book will also indirectly address other forms like age, experience, learning style, and belief. I do not claim to be an expert by any means, but my hope is that, just as I embarked on a reflective journey of my own beliefs, you will be open to doing the same.

Understanding
Diversity

CONFRONTING MY THINKING ON DIVERSITY

Typically, when people hear the word *diversity,* they tend to think of it through the lens of their own meaning. I will admit to doing that as well. I am a woman of color, yet initially, I only considered diversity from the lens of race. In other words, in a room dominated by young, white males, I almost always saw the lack of people of color before seeing that there were very few women. In my mind, I "saw" women but accepted that maybe they were not a part of this conversation. At the same token, when I was a classroom teacher in a room full of administrators, I was very aware that there were no other teachers.

After reflecting on my thoughts and discussing with several other educators, it became apparent that it is likely many of us approach diversity in much of the same way. If we are to have any chance at confronting our actions, we must first acknowledge our own inherent beliefs.

DEFINING DIVERSE VOICES

By definition, diversity alludes to a collection of differences. We are accustomed to having diverse classrooms, yet the decisions concerning what happens in those classrooms are often not made from a diverse space. In some cases, school technology decisions are not even made by a person with classroom experience. I get that this is a district decision, but to allude to the idea that a person who has worked in an EdTech company understands the needs of a classroom full of diverse learners is questionable thinking.

With that said, we must also acknowledge that just because a person has been in a classroom does not mean that they are fully present in the overall needs of a school. When it comes to technology, decisions should never be made on the backs of one small, like-minded group but on the soles of the knowledge and experiences of many. Why is this important? Multiple perspectives lend themselves to varied ideas, and it is in those ideas where we have a better chance of engaging in discussions leading to more equitable decisions.

If I were to place meaning on *diverse voices* concerning EdTech, it would be that those making the decision not only mirror the diversity of the school but also represent a collection of knowledge, beliefs, and experiences with the goal of meeting the needs of learners first. This group should not just be an administrator or administrative central office staff but should certainly include students, parents, teachers, and any interested members of the school community.

Why Diversity Matters

When it comes to learning and technology, it is important that we consider the views of many and the impact on our learners. What comes to mind for me are the schools serving a majority of students of poverty that lack the same access as schools within the district that do not. Simultaneously, the school that serves students of poverty may have access but to tools that do not effectively support its population. I cannot tell you the number of times that I have heard, "We can't give them devices because they might break, steal, or sell them," while watching truckloads head to students in other places.

Diversity matters because with understanding comes intentional thought. A single person or group of non-diverse decision makers without an understanding of their learners decides based on the lens of their own view. They tend to look at scenarios from the scope of numbers and not need. On the other hand, a group that reflects the differences of the impacted learners as well as a collection of varying yet open ideas will almost always address the needs first to align with the numbers. Diversity matters in EdTech because not all tools, devices, apps, and ideas are created equally— nor are learners.

CHAPTER 1 REFLECTIONS

- What are the demographics of your classroom, school or district?
- What are your beliefs concerning the community that you serve?
- How might those beliefs impact your decisions?
- Are your personal beliefs aligned so that the technological needs of your learners are met?
- Are students, parents, and teachers included in school EdTech decisions?

Teacher Voice in EdTech

A few years ago, my district technology department decided to standardize every classroom with a specific learning management system (LMS). It was a platform made available through our Web-filtering service, which also correlated to our active directory. This meant that student log-ins were pre-created to match their school log-ins, and creating classes was just as simple. While this sounded good on paper, the system had major flaws in terms of accessibility. At a time when we were beginning to embrace the idea of connectedness, the district-chosen system seemed to be more about shielding learners than providing them access to the world.

Many of the teachers and students in our school were actually using a different platform that had a cleaner interface and was much simpler to use. We were told, in no uncertain terms, that the district strongly discouraged its use and that, if we were to create a social learning environment, it could only be through the district-chosen system as it was one that was district managed and monitored. What was painfully obvious was that this decision, like many, was made on the basis of what was easiest at the top than what was best for kids. Furthermore, this ordeal sent a strong message to teachers that, not only did our input not matter, but we also had no choices when it came to technology.

-------------- Vignette: The Voice of the Teacher Is Critica

Aimee Bartis is passionate about serving teachers and helps them integrate technology into their existing standards in meaningful ways. Aimee is a certified technology applications teacher, librarian, and gifted educator. She writes from the perspective of her classroom below.

I remember arriving to my classroom and seeing a box on my desk . . . a new gadget. It was an Apple TV, the latest and greatest thing that was guaranteed to transform learning. I moved the box and checked for any information regarding this new purchase. I didn't find a note about the Apple TV, but I did find that the district also purchased new software. In addition, our new assistant principal planned to swing by to see the new technology in action because, like most purchases, figuring it out was an expectation for classroom teachers.

Don't get me wrong; I wasn't upset about receiving new technology. What bothered me was that I was not consulted before such a purchase was made. I could have told our technology purchasers that our network infrastructure was not prepared for Apple TV or that kids did not have the devices to interact. Maybe that was important. As for the software, I could have helped our district save thousands of dollars in licensing because we didn't need to spend money on software when kids could have accomplished the same tasks using free tools from the Web. It's rare that classroom teachers are consulted, but it most certainly should not be.

BARRIERS TO TEACHER VOICE

One of the greatest barriers to teacher voice in EdTech is perception, and that is not just on the backs of campus leaders and administrators but on how teachers think of themselves. I was teaching a training session a few weeks ago, and one teacher walked in and immediately expressed that she could not do the task. That was before she even sat at a computer. As we worked and she understood the functionality of the tool, she immediately began to design activities. She giddily talked about how much her students would enjoy the platform that we were using and ended up creating the most fantastic final product of the session. She also left that room with more than 10 different ways to integrate it into her classroom. This teacher's perception was that she could offer zero input because she did not know the tool, but she did understand her students, content, and learning strategies, which is all that she really needed to begin with.

As technology leaders, even when we say, "It's not about the tool," we often place more weight on knowledge of the tool when it comes to teachers. If we truly believe that content comes first, we have to lean more toward the skills and resources that define great teaching. When we connect with teachers on those levels, we can better understand their needs and blend in the understanding of the technology. Confidence is key, but perception of understanding is everything.

TEACHERS' PERCEPTIONS OF TECHNOLOGY

Teachers have their own opinions when it comes to technology. Some educators freely embrace the relationship that exists between technology and learning, while others are more comfortable away from the digital space.

There are typically four types of teachers in schools when it comes to technology.

1. The *Tech-Fearless Educator* takes pride in learning about new tools and ideas. This educator doesn't wait on permission to

learn but does so of his or her own free will. The tech-fearless educator is either an official or unofficial technology leader on campus and may even present at conferences. If this educator does not have access to the tools needed for learning, he or she knows exactly who to contact and takes the necessary steps to get the job done. As a matter of fact, before districts can even think about asking for input, the tech-fearless educator has already made him- or herself heard. This educator is also more than likely connected.

2. The *Tech-Compliant Educator* doesn't ask questions about what tools he or she receives. He or she attends trainings but rarely leads them. As long as there are well-written instructions or visible examples, the tech-compliant educator will use the tools in the classrooms as intended. This is the educator who is eagerly awaiting the release of district trainings when offered or relying on the release of handouts and session details from online contributors. The tech-compliant educator may be connected, but the extent of his or her connectedness is either minimal or mirrors that of his or her learning at school. In other words, the tech-compliant educator doesn't share ideas but waits patiently to receive them.

3. The *Tech-Reluctant Educator* is hindered by fear. He or she attends trainings as required but often leaves with zero buy-in as training is usually a struggle. This educator may even have classroom devices, but they are locked away in a cabinet collecting dust. If given an opportunity to add input, the tech-reluctant educator is often not heard and not because no one is listening but because he or she more than likely could not figure out how to click the link to respond. This does not mean that the tech-reluctant educator doesn't use technology at all. He or she uses it in his or her own personal space to satisfy his or her own interests but has yet to see the correlation for use in the classroom.

4. The *Anti-Everything Educator* wants absolutely nothing to do with technology or any form of change for that matter. Unfortunately, this educator is heard the most because he or she

is often voicing negative opinions to anyone who will listen. The goal of the anti-everything teacher is to disrupt progress, and we must be mindful of that.

As we move forward with trying to incorporate more teacher voice in our campus technology decisions, we must fully understand each of these types of teachers and what drives these kinds of thinking. Just because a teacher will do as asked with no questions doesn't mean that we should not purposefully seek their input. At the same token, just because a teacher is reluctant doesn't mean that he or she can't be engaged. With that said, you cannot force a person to offer input in discussions where he or she is not interested, but you might be surprised at who wants to be heard when he or she is given the platform to speak.

Teacher Tech Type Reflections

1. Are you tech-fearless, tech-compliant, tech-reluctant, or anti-everything?
2. How does each of these teacher types impact student learning?
3. What can teachers do to become more fearless?

CAMPUS LEADERS: DEVELOPING TEACHER TECH LEADERS

As a classroom teacher, I definitely would have described myself as a tech-fearless educator. I've always enjoyed exploring to learn and definitely embraced that in my own teaching and learning. Any opportunity that I had to either train other teachers or serve on decision-making committees, I jumped at, which helped me to swiftly develop as a leader.

In thinking of my own experiences, I have to wonder if we are in fact offering teachers on our campuses the opportunities to do the same. In other words, are we creating an environment in which teachers feel that they not only have a voice but a platform in which to grow? Are we creating a community of developers or a community that needs development?

Ideas for Developing Teacher Tech Leaders on Campus

1. **Don't make the fearless-tech teacher your only go-to for all things technology.** When you do this, you are creating an environment of only them instead of us too. The fearless-tech teacher is one of your greatest assets in terms of willingness to tackle new ideas, but we must be careful that, as we continuously validate the ideas of the teachers with automatic buy-in, we don't inadvertently invalidate the others. Many teachers will not automatically jump at the chance to share because they don't realize that what they are doing in their classrooms is in fact transformative. As you see those moments, encourage those teachers to share with their team or even staff.

2. **Have an unconference led by your campus teachers.** What I love most about Edcamps is that they are 100 percent driven by the collective knowledge of the group. An unconference isn't about the "star" of the room but about amplifying what participants want to learn and their comfort in leading the learning. This is an excellent way to help teachers become more confident leaders, which will only further the cause when it comes to technology. In addition, this is a great way to pose an open discussion where teachers can freely voice their technology concerns.

3. **Have an open policy for when teachers want to teach official campus training.** This should be a priority. When teachers want to lead training, they should be given the platform to do so. Yes, your fearless educator may be compelled to lead sessions as much as possible, but by encouraging teachers to be collaborative, they will only gain more through developing together.

4. **Encourage your teachers to submit proposals to speak at conferences.** As a frequent conference attendee and presenter,

I actually love hearing from teachers who are currently in practice versus a specialist who is not. In addition, it is a proven fact that, when a teacher or trainer is faced with sharing with a broader audience, he or she almost always becomes an even stronger expert of the content he or she is teaching.

5. **Form a committee to explore campus technology goals, and give teachers ownership of ensuring that goals are met.** This option is like killing two birds with one stone. Teachers not only get to lead a charge but have a voice in its development. For campuses that are in charge of their own technology purchases in lieu of a district office, this is huge.

6. **Get teachers connected.** As cliché as it may sound, being connected can be a game changer for anyone with a vested interest in education, especially teachers. Through social media, teachers will not only have access to the global dynamics of classrooms but also to learning events that are not often communicated about in school. While Twitter is not the only platform for connectedness, it is one of the most widely used.

TEACHER VOICE IN TECHNOLOGY PROFESSIONAL DEVELOPMENT

When I started my career, I did not have a say in the menu of courses that my district taught. We logged into a training system and chose, based on what was being provided. The problem was that none of the provided sessions applied to what I needed, and when district requirements were that a certain number of hours be earned through in-district training, it meant that a large majority of teachers were taking courses just to earn the hours. That was more than 10 years ago, and sadly, in many school districts, this is still the case.

While I do agree that there are certain elements of technology that teachers are sometimes unaware of, I also believe that, if we are asking teachers to serve students according to their needs, we must engage teachers and serve their needs the same. What does this mean? For starters, aside from the district-identified critical technology pieces, teachers must be given an avenue to provide input on what they learn as well as how they learn it.

Within our connected community, we have come to understand the value of the Edcamp model, and many conversations have occurred concerning how to implement such an idea at the school district level. What if the powers that be who coordinate the district technology training plan started with a question as simple as "What do you want to learn" and then planned accordingly? Think of it as a needs assessment compiling data directly from the end users.

I've seen countless discussions about teachers not knowing enough to decipher what they need to know, and in many cases, this is an accurate description. How does one gain input from a teacher who has no idea what to ask for? It can be done, but that means that we, as technology coaches and trainers, must be prepared to do the one thing that we often struggle with the most—listen.

A few days ago, I walked into a meeting with a group of teachers during their planning period. I made it quite clear that I was not there to teach them any tools during their planning time. I was there to observe and learn from them. As a matter of fact, I wasn't listening for specific mentions of technology. Instead, I was listening for intended outcomes as this too is data.

Knowing what teachers wanted to accomplish for themselves and their students was critical to thinking through the addition of application technology. Teachers may not have been able to verbalize what they wanted to learn, but hearing them speak about creativity, collaboration, critical thinking, and communication opened doors for discussion that would not have been possible had I not had the frame of mind to leave my agenda outside while engulfing myself into their processes. With that said, I am not blind to a certain truth about teachers not knowing what it is that they do not know. However, this same idea applies to anyone in a coaching position because, until we can learn to listen before acting, we won't know what teachers know either.

This past year, during her International Society for Teacher Education (ISTE) Ignite Speech, Jenny Magiera, a brilliant educator from Chicago, spoke on this very idea about teachers owning their own professional development. She talked about teachers taking back professional development through an individual exploration plan, which embeds teacher-driven goals, reflections, and critical questions about how technology impacts student learning. Professional development is not a one-off event and most certainly should not be about being on the receiving end of a list of apps void of purpose. If we aren't including teachers in their own learning starting with their goals, who are we serving beyond our own strengths in teaching?

If you still have the mind-set that teachers cannot provide valid input into their own learning goals when it comes to technology, here are a couple of ideas.

1. **Create a resource page that includes more than links to apps and what they do.** Connect with your own network, and post videos and reflections from other teachers and students centered on content with great pedagogy where the tool is supporting learning. A teacher who is unfamiliar with a certain idea will gravitate toward seeing it in action and will more than likely want to know more.

2. **Use district technology initiatives to your advantage.** Plant seeds, and questions will follow. For example, many of our English language arts (ELA) teachers are using Google docs for writing. When I'm with teachers, I always make a point to share, collaborate, and use something like research tools. It is my favorite seed to plant because teachers love it and then bombard me with requests for additional training, which means that we can visit other uses that they had no idea existed.

3. **Center training on the four Cs (Collaboration, Creativity, Critical Thinking, Communication), dressed in content and not on tools.** Leave the tools open-ended, and use them as needed to accomplish the task. If teachers need additional training that is more tool specific, encourage them to

communicate this on their feedback forms and follow up.

4. **Provide multiple means of learning.** This should be a given. Every piece trained should have virtual as well as face-to-face offerings. Many services package unlimited access to various platforms for virtual learning, but in my opinion, just as teachers are encouraged to place their lessons online, so should be technology coaches and trainers.

5. **Collect feedback often, and act on it.** Every training session should include a space for feedback and a simple form on a website where teachers can make suggestions and requests and even submit their own sessions to teach as warranted. When teachers offer feedback, use that information to improve their professional learning experiences, including your own methods.

CHAPTER 2 REFLECTIONS

- How are you including teacher voice in your school or district when it comes to technology?
- Where exactly do teachers fit into the equation when it comes to major purchasing decisions involving classroom tools?
- What barriers to teacher voice exist in your school or district environment? How will you address them?

CHAPTER 3

The Student Learner Perspective

Braxton, a former student, considers herself very connected. She's constantly using her phone and considers it just as important as the clothes on her back. Her phone connects her to the world. She talks about a day of her connected life in the classroom below.

I wake up in the morning and check my phone to see which day it is at school, an A day or B day. I do this because I keep the details of my assignments in my calendar. I have a Spanish project due today, and even though I begged to use some apps on my phone to do my project, my teacher would not agree to it. Instead, she made us do a 20-slide PowerPoint. I took a design class this summer, so as she gave us the

(Continued)

(Continued)

assignment, I cringed. She actually wanted full paragraphs on each slide. Who does that? She also said that we could not use Google translate, and if we did, she would know. I've used it all year and made As on all of my assignments, so this made me laugh.

I wanted to do a video instead and speak Spanish. I even told her that I could put subtitles in my video, which would show her that I not only understood the language in written form but could also speak it. She said that she had been doing this assignment for 10 years and that she did not have a rubric to grade a video. Is this real life? My English teacher has no problem with negotiating projects and loves my ideas. She's even used some of them in her other classes. Why is this teacher different?

Unlike my friends in other districts, my school does not have devices for students, and even though we have open Wi-Fi, we can't bring our own devices. As a matter of fact, if a teacher sees me using my phone in class, he or she can tell me to put it away or take it and turn it into the office. Our school policy does allow phones to be used in the classroom as long as the teacher is using them for learning. Even though none of my teachers are using phones in this way, I do have two teachers that understand my need to organize and will allow me to place my assignments in my phone. My other teachers are not so open. I've even suggested that they have a website or even Tweet out the assignments. Clearly, this was language more foreign than my Spanish class.

I will graduate next year, and had it not been for my own interest in technology, I would be behind. I'm probably behind already. It kills me to have to power down so much at school, and if my principal and teachers would listen, many of us could teach them how to change some of these assignments to include technology as simple as a cell phone. Then again, they would have to stop taking them away first. They also should understand that we are using them anyway.

STUDENTS HAVE IDEAS TOO

In schools, adults tend to make all of the decisions on behalf of the people that they impact most, students. We tell them what technology they have to use and even specify the apps, if applicable. If students are allowed to be creative, it is too often the result of a massive negotiation. When I read Braxton's story, I cringed in so many places because this was a student who understood her needs. This was a student who was well versed in how she learned, and yet this student was denied the right to create what would have been a more powerful demonstration of learning.

We all know teachers in our buildings who are this way

> When we use our power to hinder student growth, we all lose.

regardless of the administrative restrictions that are in place. With that said, a restricted campus almost certainly guarantees to produce a closed-minded teacher, which means that student creativity is also stifled. I like how Braxton ended her piece with saying that students were using their devices anyway because they are, and maybe we should listen.

Student Ideas for Mobile Devices

Because Braxton was so determined to use her mobile device in class, I asked her for some ideas to pass on to teachers. She is a high school senior, so some of her suggestions far exceed the sites that are open in most schools. However, the gist of her ideas can be used in other forms.

- **Visual Learning With Instagram:** Students use Instagram for everything. Using images, we can overlay quotes, poetry, or small writings and use the comment section for even more information. We can share them, comment to each other, and make our work searchable using a hashtag. Many teachers use this app already too, so it should be easy to learn.

- **Twitter Discussions:** In so many classes, we've had to watch videos and complete discussion questions. We could do this using Twitter, which would also mean that everyone will participate because we're already secretly using Twitter while watching the video. So, instead of Tweeting how bored we are, we could be discussing what we are seeing and also connecting with each other because, right now, we do not.

- **Create and Edit Videos:** I make videos that tell stories for Instagram through apps on my phone. I even have an app that lets me put video with pictures. Short videos can produce large results, and they are simple to do. Teachers do not need to teach us to do this because, for those that do not know, there are many students who do and will share.

- **Snapchat Stories:** We collect images and videos for an extended period of time and share them in one string of stories through Snapchat. When I collaborate with my peers, this is how we do it. While I cannot turn these in for a grade, they are fun to spark ideas, and those ideas can be utilized for other things. Yes, I know that it is blocked in most schools, so this may not be something that works for every classroom, but it's an idea that works for students.

- **Blogging:** I blog with an app on my phone, and if the goal is to develop students to be more reflective and think critically, we should all be blogging. Most of us are using Tumblr for personal updates. If Tumblr is not an option, students are open to any form of online communication. At some point, students must be trusted enough to communicate appropriately, and if not, we can learn.

STUDENT VOICE AND EDTECH

A few months ago, I visited another district where all students had district-issued devices. What I loved about this particular school was that, although the district provided them, students could also opt to bring their own. Many students chose this route because they knew that the district device would not serve the majority of their needs.

Another district that I visited actually gave students multiple district-issued choices. They did this by setting up a room where students and parents came in to test devices before making a final decision. In this school, upon graduation, the device ownership turns over to the student. While this may seem like a small gesture considering the life span of devices, students and parents were excited about it. As a matter of fact, this became an option only after students made the suggestion.

We also have the situation such as in Braxton's school, where students are not only denied a choice in terms of tools, but they are denied the tools themselves. Much of that, as stated earlier, is due to policy, yet so much of it is a result of teacher understanding. We block what we do not understand, yet we make no effort in trying. So much good can come from not only having open discussions with kids but also in learning from them. By the way, revisiting the "Developing Teacher Tech Leaders" section from Chapter 2, should also include this new option: Learn from students.

THREE SIMPLE SOLUTIONS FOR ENGAGING STUDENT VOICE

1. **Make assignments more open-ended and less prescriptive.** Instead of telling kids to complete an assignment with a certain app, give them a rubric with the intended outcome, and let them choose the path to get there. By doing this, you are not only empowering them to let their creativity shine, but you will also learn something from them in the process. For those students who will struggle with this idea, you can have some examples, but a better idea may be to incorporate tools like Google groups or Padlet to curate resources. This also places ownership of learning in the hands of students.

2. **Create an environment that welcomes student ideas.** If you aren't going to be open to less-prescriptive assignments, at least be open to their suggestions when they have another way. If one of our goals is to help students become better critical

thinkers, collaborators, and communicators, this is important because they certainly utilize all of these skills in sharing their ideas with you and their peers.

3. **Make sure that your teaching style is inviting and not alienating.** While this may not sound like it impacts student voice, it does. We have to be careful not to create an environment that only encourages the free thinking of our top students but one that reaches our least communicable as well. Encourage students to share, and do it often because the most marginalized of students will often not shine without feeling that they have permission to do so. Even then, you have to work harder to amplify their ideas.

THE MISSING VOICE OF STUDENTS OF POVERTY

For more than a year, I've participated in many online Twitter chats with topics ranging from bring your own technology (BYOT) to apps for various devices. In isolation, through other communities, I've engaged in multiple conversations regarding reaching students of poverty. Unfortunately, the intersection between EdTech and conversations regarding poverty has yet to occur. As a matter of fact, when extensive conversations regarding poverty have taken place, the missing voices seemed to be the majority of members of the EdTech community, which led me to believe one of four things at any given time.

1. Students of poverty were nonexistent in schools where most EdTech conversationalists worked.

2. Conversations regarding poverty were not as appealing as apps and devices when it came to stats and measuring trending conversations.

3. There really was a perception out there that all students, even those of poverty, had immediate access to online information and tools.

4. The general consensus among EdTech conversationalists was that there was no real solution regarding students of poverty.

Any combination of these thoughts does nothing to change the fact that we have kids in schools that lack equitable access as their peers. Even if schools are providing devices, is it fair to ask the homeless kid, struggling to understand where his or her evening meal is going to come from, to head to McDonald's to access a flipped lesson? If schools are utilizing BYOT, is it a fair assumption that all kids have smartphones with data plans or Wi-Fi capabilities? Is it fair to think that, even with devices, students have free time at home to fulfill project requirements?

Vignette: I Didn't Have a Choice but to Work Night Shift

My father left home when I was nine. I watched my mom work two jobs to take care of me and my five brothers and sisters. As soon as I was old enough to work, I knew that I had to get a job. The only place that would hire me and pay enough to help feed my family and take care of bills was a factory. The schedule that they offered me was a third shift, where I worked from 11 p.m. to 7 a.m. I couldn't afford not to take the job, even though I had to be at school by 8:30 a.m.

School was hard. I could barely keep my eyes open in class. My teachers would get mad because I never had my homework. They didn't understand that I barely had time to sleep. One teacher even told me that it was my choice to work. I didn't have a choice. If I didn't work, we didn't eat. Some of my teachers did try to help. They put their lessons online so that I could watch them. It's too bad that I didn't have Internet access. They told me that I could come early to school and watch them in the library. I was barely making it to school by 8:30 a.m., so that didn't work. I graduated, and to this day, I can't tell you how. It's been five years, and I still work at the same factory. My name is Hector, and this is all I know how to do.

TECHNOLOGY FOR STUDENTS
WITH NO CHOICE

Hector's story is one that is common for many students at the secondary level. This is a kid who had all odds against him. He didn't have access to tools, information, or time. On most days, I found this kid in the office with a referral for his sleeping in class or "refusal" to complete assignments. In Hector's case, a little understanding would have gone a long way. This was a kid who desired success but lacked the means of achieving it. He had no advocates for his success beyond creating shortcuts to pacify his requirements.

The consistent quick fix for Hector and other students like him was to eject him from mainstream school and send him to an outside program created to cater to students who needed flexible school schedules. On the surface, this sounded perfect because Hector could then work his third shift and attend school from 12 p.m. to 4 p.m. He would sign in to a computer and take all of his courses online. It was a program modeled much like the factory that encompassed his nights. He could click through a series of multiple-choice assessments to graduate, which is exactly what he did.

This quick-fix approach accomplished one task only. Hector received his high school diploma but not much else. With all odds against him, school provided him no outlet. The technology that was supposed to provide access provided nothing more than a faster track to where he is today, trapped in the city limits of his hometown, working in a factory, and longing for a better life. Where is the equity in that?

The one voice missing in Hector's story is his own. Had any decision maker bothered asking Hector what he wanted to accomplish, he would have told them that he wanted to try to go to college. He would have told them that he wanted to continue to push himself so that he could in fact have a chance at a different life. Instead, his future was sold to him as an "easier way to get through school so that he could focus on work." Part of me understands this thinking, but the other part of me wishes that he had the courage to speak up for himself when no one else could.

The easiest choice, when it comes to technology, is not always the best choice. Yet, for students like Hector and others in similar situations, "easy" seems to prevail over all logic, including the voice of those that it impacts most—students.

CHAPTER 3 REFLECTIONS

1. Does your school or district have policies in place that are actually inhibiting learning?
2. What can we do to develop our teachers so that they can be more open to student ideas such as Braxton's?
3. How are your students using technology, and how can you incorporate their natural use of these tools into the learning environment?
4. What are you doing to address device equity and access needs in your school?
5. What options do you have available for students like Hector, whose needs often exceed the plans that many schools have in place?
6. In a sea of technology initiatives, how are you making sure that the voices of students with no access are heard and that they too are given innovative opportunities to learn?

CHAPTER

4

Beyond Pencil Skirts and High Heels

Women of EdTech

Vignette: I Started With a Why . . .
I Continue for the Who

Lisa Johnson has 12 years of educational experience ranging from teaching high school English and math to international curriculum development, creating and presenting workshops, and even running technology integration camps across the state of Texas. Currently, Lisa serves Eanes Independent School District (ISD), which proudly supports a 1:1 iPad initiative from Kindergarten through grade 12. Additionally, she has been recognized and selected as an Apple Distinguished Educator. Inspired by author Simon Sinek, Lisa (@techchef4u) shares a piece of her journey into educational technology below.

(Continued)

(Continued)

The first year of iPads was a tough one—it felt like a futile endeavor to manage them, and truly, very few educators had any idea what to do with them beyond basic consumptive tasks (e.g., online research, educational games, etc.). I wanted to change that. I wanted to show my teachers the transformative power of the device for creativity and student products and began crafting my own one-page iPad lessons. At the time, all I had was a teacher website, and I found it severely ineffective for organizing content and resources for teachers.

But beyond that, I knew that I would not be in the district I was working for forever, and I wanted to be able to expand upon the work and ideas I had cultivated while working there. When a teacher leaves a district, typically all of his or her internal Web pages are shut down— lights out on all the ideas and impact. I felt very strongly that I wanted to ensure that the work and resources I created and curated continued to be available for those teachers within the district as well as anyone else who would like them. So I started a "rogue" WordPress blog and began sharing and blogging. Three hundred posts later, my blogs and writing had evolved. At the time I began blogging, there was very little educational content available on the Web to support purposeful iPad integration, so when I found a gem or two, I wanted to retain them for later reference. Pinterest seemed the best tool at the time to archive this information, so I began pinning iPad lessons. Little did I know then that the resource that I initially curated for myself would be a top hit in Google, housing more than 1,800 iPad lessons and impacting 16,000 educators around the world.

But that wasn't enough. I found that many educators at the time continued to struggle with utilizing iPads to support meaningful, product-based instruction, so I teamed up with Yolanda Barker, a colleague in the district, to coauthor the free iBook *Hot Apps 4 HOTS*. Rather than retain the book for district-use only, we sought to push the envelope and have it published to the iBookstore. With more than 20,000 international downloads, I am thankful that we made the decision to share beyond district lines. Seeking to meet the needs of a diverse group of adult learners, Yolanda and I teamed up once again to cohost a weekly podcast, "Appy Hours 4 U," devoted to sharing instructional integration ideas for apps and meeting the needs of busy educators that thrived on professional development in their PJ's.

An Apple representative, multiple Twitter chats, and a site visit to WHS 1:1 iPad pilot led me to leave my current district and make the leap, with my entire family in tow, to embark on a journey with the iVengers, our EdTech team, and Kindergarten through grade 12 1:1 initiative. Later that year, I was honored as an Apple Distinguished Educator for my work over the past three years with iPads in education.

The latest numbers published by the National Center for Women in Information Technology show that only 26 percent of computer-related jobs are held by women. Of that 26 percent, 56 percent of them leave the profession. While those numbers are staggering, let's think about the fact that, of the 26 percent employed in computer-related jobs, only 4 percent of those are in leadership. To say that there is a disparity in the influence of women in EdTech is an understatement. Thinking that this data does not directly impact education is a mistake.

> While I may have started with the why (e.g., the need for purposeful and meaningful examples and support for iPad integration within the K–12 sector), I continue the journey for the students whom this work impacts and the teachers whom this work inspires.

This summer, as I was examining the job boards for school technology leadership positions, I noticed a trend in required background knowledge for almost every job. Each posting seemed to echo the same sentiments, that is, that experience in EdTech business leadership was preferred. Most schools, for chief technology officer (CTO) or technology director jobs, preferred to hire from the world of corporate technology, which sounds great in terms of business and infrastructure until the data regarding women in those fields is considered. What does the pool of candidates look like for school technology leadership positions? I'll give you a hint. There are not enough women in consideration.

When I started my career in education, I was fortunate to work in a school where a woman held the technology director position, and I credit her with providing the pathway that led me to technology. She not only came from an educational background but also understood the necessities of being more intentionally diverse. She didn't just buy products for classrooms but opened the table of opinion for others to contribute. I appreciated that very much because, through her leadership, I was able to be at the forefront of conversations gaining insightful knowledge in the areas of planning, implementation, training, and development.

I would love to say that watching a woman in leadership was exceptional at all times. Unfortunately, that was not always the case. There were moments where I witnessed a certain lack of support on behalf of both men and women. I heard her referred to in words that no man would ever be called. People questioned her decisions just as much as they trusted her input, and that often accompanied references to sexist remarks that were both inappropriate and unbelievable. Those were the ugly moments for sure, but watching her work with her head held high, undeterred by the negativity, is something that still sits within my vision today.

That was years ago, and as much as I would love to say that times have changed, in many places, this is often not the case. When schools and districts have women who are ready to offer ideas and critical input and lead, we must make sure that internal systems are not prohibitive but are designed for discussions that not only encourage equitable input but demand it. We must also make sure that we value women for their technical expertise just as much as their pedagogical knowledge.

In other words, if school spaces are not open to the idea that women are just as capable of outlining a network infrastructure or troubleshooting a computer as we are at writing curriculum, then that space is not one that values the full breadth of knowledge that women can bring to the table. If you are wondering about your own space, think of the men and women in your technology department. Who gets the call when it comes to instructional design versus technical understanding? Hopefully, there are women involved, and if there are not, it is time to question why.

We need more women in educational technology roles, not just for the purpose of satisfying a call for diversity but because we offer points of view, processes, and insight that are different. We also offer presence in a field that is hurting to attract more girls into its ranks. What better way to encourage more girls to study technology than to empower the women who are in a position to influence them?

CONNECTED WOMEN AS SERIOUS VOICES OF TECH INFLUENCE

When it comes to women in school technology, there are often embedded barriers to voice through leadership due to hiring practices but also a systemic barrier to voice through influence due to lack of opportunity to lead from the inside. That doesn't mean that women have to be silent observers. We are teachers, after all. What this means is that sometimes we have to chart our own paths, push against barriers, take more risks, and develop ourselves as experts of what we know that works. We are also present at a time in which sharing what we do is critical.

In 2013, I attended the Edtechwomen dinner at ISTE in San Antonio, Texas. Edtechwomen, an organization founded by Sehreen NoorAli (@sehreentech) and Margaret Roth (@teachingdaisy), was inspired by the influence of women in education. They recognized that, even with a plethora of opportunities for women in educational technology, educator voice, awareness, and visibility were simply not there. This event was my first time connecting with women across an entire ecosystem of technological experiences where we shared our concerns and triumphs openly.

For years, all that we have ever heard about women in EdTech was that there was a definite shortage and that women are often not the ones leading innovative change. I felt empowered sitting shoulder to shoulder with other educators, developers, chief executive officers (CEOs), directors, programmers, and EdTech writers. I had no idea that so many women were not only in positions of leadership in their respective fields but also directly developing products for our classrooms. I felt empowered at hearing how our input impacted their development. More importantly, I learned that, even when we struggle with invoking change in our schools, we have the power to impact classrooms on a grander scale through our social connections.

I am fortunate to have connected with a large number of amazing women in technology through Twitter and various networks. Through weekly educational chats, we have shared our instructional ideas, classroom experiences, and pro tips concerning meaningful integration. We also engaged in discussions about the lack of leadership opportunities for women and how to reach success when the gender odds are against us. Those were the moments that influenced my decision to transition from math curriculum to technology integration. I've worked in environments throughout my career where I was the only woman in the room, so this move should have been a piece of cake. If only it were that simple.

For me, the transition to technology was challenging. There were highs and lows, with most of those lows centered on the fact that, even though I had a seat at the decision-making table, I often felt stifled of my own voice. As confident as I am in my own life, I sometimes felt inadequate. I found myself being a bit more silent as if I were waiting for permission to think. As I talked with many of my Edtechwomen peers through social media, I learned that my muted thoughts were similar to how others felt.

In our perfect online existence, we were the voices of change in our networks. In our schools, we were often void of input. The more that we talked through online and offline mediums, the more that we began to talk through common issues and empowered each other. This is why a PLN is critical.

Even when we are the only women in the room, we are never alone. When we are charged with developing some idea, someone connected to us has not only done it but shared it and will share the process. When we are struggling to rid ourselves of silence, someone is waiting in the wings with a bullhorn in tow. When we are ready to tackle the next step in our careers toward technology leadership, there's an embedded network of support to help navigate the process. The gender odds may not be in our favor, but experience and influence speak volumes. This is our greatest power as connected school technologists.

This is our greatest power as women.

EMPOWERING EDTECH WOMEN LEADERS AT SCHOOL

One of the questions that I am asked most often is about how I got to this point in my career. It was definitely not an overnight process, and many doors were opened for me along the way, starting with my first technology director giving me the opportunity to lead and evaluate effectiveness of classroom technology. The second door was my second principal putting me in charge of every aspect of our school technology plan from contract negotiations, district presentations, installation, and development, to the implementation of our professional development process.

Opportunities are not solely based on what you do but are also based on your influence to inspire others. As a woman in school technology, this is almost always true. As someone who is finally at the point in my career where my voice is directly heard, I fully understand the need to include and empower more women to be a part of the process. Below are a few key points that helped make my transition to this EdTech dream a reality.

- **Brand Yourself:** Some of the greatest questions that anyone has ever asked me were, "What can you teach me, and where are you sharing it? What is your expertise?" I started my blog because of these questions.

- **Mentor Other Teachers:** Don't keep your ideas to yourself. Share them, and offer to follow up through reflection. This is important as it helps to develop additional leadership skills that will come in handy along the way. You can also help teachers become more growth minded, and that will build a sense of professional self in them.

- **Do Your Research:** You have to stay on top of trends whether good or bad because your voice may just be the only one in the room to remind that group of mostly men that flipping the classroom and BYOT both present problems when a majority of your students are of poverty and lack access. Research forces us to think in other ways, and you can bring that to the table.

- **Share Your Expertise Globally:** If you plan to be a leader in school, it's also important to contribute to the global community. This will also help you to bounce ideas on others, reflect, and adjust when needed.

- **Build Relationships With EdTech Companies Developing Products for Schools:** Your inside connections will help you to communicate ideas for change quicker, check on updates, and address issues personally. This is not meant to be a point of bragging or loyalty to a brand. This is meant to give you firsthand access on having a say in the technology that is going in your classrooms or schools.

- **Present at Regional, State, and National Conferences:** Your résumé matters, but so does your commitment to professional learning opportunities. Presenting at conferences shows your commitment to research and sharing best practices. It also helps to establish your expertise in the field. In addition, these events are often absent of the voice of women, and your presenting helps to change that. When you have the floor, be prepared to speak up because my doing that is why you are reading this thought right now.

- **Seek Career-Related Honors:** I will be the first one to say that I cringe every time I have to list an award or honor, but I also recognize that, whether we like it or not, they open doors that would otherwise be closed.

The most important tip that I cannot stress enough is that you must share. Had I not shared every aspect of my career online from lesson reflections to the implementation of new ideas, that second door would not have been opened. Without that opportunity, I would not have been in the position that I am in now, that is, to bring a much-needed missing voice to my current work space.

It is imperative to note that, once you are in the position to impact direct change in your school, you advocate to make room for others. In the words of my mother, when a chair is extended to us, we are responsible for extending the next chair to the next person.

CHAPTER 4 REFLECTIONS

1. What are you doing in your school or district to encourage more EdTech leadership among women?
2. What role does mentorship play in encouraging other women to find their voices?
3. What are the implications of denying the contributions of women in discussions concerning classroom technology?
4. What role does connectedness play in the development of the tech-fearless women in your school?

CHAPTER
5

The Unspoken Inequity

People of Color in EdTech

Rachelle Wooten is a wife and mother of five children. She works as an educational technology specialist in suburban Houston. She enjoys researching, coaching, writing, and presenting at conferences.

In my diverse school district in southwest Houston, I have grown accustomed to seeing people of color on any one of our more than 70 campuses. I had no idea that this was not the norm as this is my normal. When I attended our statewide conference and connected with a few other technologists of color, I was taken aback at how many of us are not in diverse schools and how many of them were the first people of color in theirs. As we dug deeper into the schools that were represented day after day, we wondered why more people of color

(Continued)

(Continued)

were not directly involved with their school or district technology progress or, if they were, why they were not present.

I have a voice in my school because of the culturally diverse environment where I live. That's not to say that others are not also in diverse environments, but I know that my voice is directly impacting the technological opportunities for children, especially those of color. I know that my presence means that others see me and understand that, not only are they represented, but they can feel the possibilities within their own voices.

In educational technology, the overlapping theme of any messenger is that of change and adaptation to embrace new ways of reaching the educators and students we serve. We speak of the need to let go of old paradigms and pedagogies in order to meet the varying, individual needs of our students. We are encouraged to get out of the box with our thinking, and we are challenged to collaborate with others so that we develop cultural awareness and engage with learners of different cultures. If that is the recurring message, then, why is there very little variation in the messengers?

There is something to be said about seeing people that look like me in school technology leadership. While we look the same, I know that we still may see the world differently, but we also share an immediate common bond that inspires and encourages me to keep breaking through, speaking up, and sharing out. When I see people that look like me leading, presenting, Tweeting, moderating, and chatting, it stirs up my sense of belonging and acceptance.

Months after the conference, I am no longer wondering. I am now committed to taking action. As a woman of color, I am on a mission to invite, mentor, and encourage others to share their expertise and experiences on this journey of education and change.

RECOGNIZING EXPERTISE AT THE SCHOOL LEVEL

As a classroom teacher, I began training teachers on innovative uses of technology before I completed my first full year as a certified teacher. This was definitely not a result of my school district reaching out to me but a result of me being in the right place at the right time. That place happened to be on the convention floor of our state conference. I was leaving a session, and as I walked towards an exit, I ran into a group from my school, including my technology director. I was a classroom teacher attending a conference that our school had traditionally sent only our technology crew to. After a bit of small talk and a few months, I was asked to share in a session for teachers, and that request was because my technology director requested it.

What I did not know then was that my earning of this opportunity was not the norm. As a matter of fact, there were no other people of color as trainers. As years passed, we did add a few more, but it was still only a few. I will never forget my first time stepping out with my district technology team as a trainer for our schools. It's been 10 years, but the looks on the faces of the teachers of color as I presented my sessions are still visible when I pause to reflect. When the session ended, one teacher, whom I knew from our community events, touched my arm and whispered, "Thank you." I asked her why she was thanking me, and she responded that she never thought she would see "one of us" teaching those classes. She encouraged me to keep doing it because I was making a difference.

It's often difficult to comprehend the magnitude of the power of seeing yourself until you are the person being seen. I was lucky enough to see other teachers stand and say, "I can do this too," and there is a small sense of pride in knowing that the door was opened for them to do so. However, it pains me to think of the number of teachers who are out there still waiting in the wings for permission to stand and be leaders among the single-race overcrowded space that we call technology.

If we are so blind that we are not recognizing the talent within our own schools, how can we expect to see any different at the state or national level that Rachelle so eloquently discussed?

With that said, I remember a fellow teacher of color pulling me aside after signing my contract to whisper what I call the worst advice that I have ever been given. She advised me that I needed to make sure to keep all of my expertise to myself. She went on to say that, if the school knew that I knew anything, they would either use me or mute me. While I did find this advice rather odd, I understood where she was coming from. The difference was that I came into education knowing that the world was much bigger than my town and my classroom and that the only way that I could continue to have access to the world was through sharing. Sharing is how opportunities that spark growth come to fruition.

On a campus or district level, it is important that we have avenues established that provide more teachers the chance to share their classrooms. We must also be purposeful in not just attracting teachers of color but encouraging them. That encouragement must extend well beyond the frame of a school but also to other schools, districts, and even states.

We have to create a culture where "not me" is void of being an option. That culture won't exist unless we create opportunities and are open to the opportunities that people of color are creating for themselves.

BREAKING CULTURAL CODE

Empowering to Share

A few months after ISTE 2013, I remember an individual questioning the number of presenters of color present in the program. I distinctly remember being annoyed at this question because, at the time, it didn't occur to me that this was something that needed to be questioned. To this day, I still regret that I did not push the issue with him further.

While denial of the technological contributions of teachers of color is very much a campus and district issue, it is critically important for campuses and districts to understand that their denial has greater implications. When campuses and districts are not empowering the voice and expertise of teachers of color, they are also controlling the flow of conversations at professional learning events when those voices are absolutely necessary yet silent. People still equate students of color to poverty, and while this is often this case, it is not always the case. What we bring to discussions is the connection and understanding of the power of access to opportunity. Technology provides that access, but best practices are not always aligned to what we know works with children of color.

When it comes to EdTech, people of color bring a much broader perspective concerning diverse learners. I bring my classroom experiences, nuances, and cultural connections that are often not explored. I remember seeing a teacher in my building craft a much-applauded, technology-rich lesson in which the characters in her video were adults of color portrayed in every negative stereotype imaginable. I looked around the room, and not one person was going to say a word as conversations about race make non-people of color uncomfortable. My voice in that room meant that there was open discussion about the cultural and ethical characterizations in that video. In addition, beyond the obvious racial implications, we could talk about how the learning styles of students of color demanded more inquiry, activity, and creation. Yes, this is true for all learners, but this is especially true for students of color.

The problem with schools teaching students of color where no teacher of color is involved in instructional decisions is that direct discussions concerning the specific needs of those students are often not discussed. Not talking about it doesn't help the students who desperately need people to understand best practices in reaching them. What happens when teachers of color are absent of sharing is that the message delivered is more one size fits all than realistically applies in our schools. This is certainly true when it comes to technology and how we view it in the learning cycle. With that said, it shouldn't be that having a person of color in the room is the only way that common-sense decisions are made. At some point, the expectation must be that we are all cognizant of how our ideas concerning other races and cultures can have impact on learners.

CONNECTING TEACHERS OF COLOR

I am fortunate to be connected to such a diverse group of educators, and I can definitely vouch for the necessity of doing so. In the last few months, I have not only connected with more teachers and school technologists of color but have built meaningful relationships where we have been able to have meaningful discussions surrounding our efforts and growth as well as offer a level of support, an earpiece, that can only be achieved through understanding from a first-person point of view.

Of the thousands of teachers that I am connected to and thousands more whom I have seen over the years in schools and at school technology events, I can only name fewer than 20 of my connections who are of color and who are also actively contributing to discussions concerning EdTech. In the technology director position, I have only met two, and neither is from my home state. That does not mean that people of color are not pursuing leadership opportunities in public education. We are. Unfortunately, we are not stepping into the arena of technology, and it has simply become normal.

The past summer, I was an Ignite speaker at ISTE, not the only person of color but the only black woman on stage. I can say that I did not fully comprehend the magnitude of that moment until days later as I connected with more teachers of color. To many, I represented something much bigger than a non-person of color would understand. I was there, and my being there meant that others felt that they could be there too. We are still at a point where paving the way is necessary, and that is a huge challenge when the way is not readily available to pave.

One of my most asked questions is how I got to the place that I am now in this field—a woman of color who is active within this technology community. Well, for starters, I stopped being silent. I recognized my own value and started sharing. This part was critical. In addition, I connected with not just teachers of color but also teachers who inspired me regardless of race and more importantly supported me. I found that, if I wanted to have a voice in where technology is headed, I needed to use mine. I needed to connect in deep, global discussions and be strong enough to stand when certain topics needed to be pushed.

My path into educational technology would not have been fully possible had it not been for people like Scott Floyd, a Texas educator who saw something in me that I did not see in myself at the time. He introduced me to a large majority of my state's EdTech community and is still encouraging me to this day. Through Scott, I connected with Steve Dembo, who then encouraged me to join the Discovery Education community, which encompasses a highly diverse group of educators who work for kids—all kids—and those connections not only opened more doors but allowed more conversations.

Earlier this year, I connected with what I call my personal support network, a group of teachers and activists known holistically as Educolor. This group, initially spearheaded by Jose Vilson, Sabrina Stevens, Melinda Anderson, Xian Barrett, Jason Buell, and Liz Dwyer, has grown to include even more diverse voices that are also focused on increasing the presence and validation of people of color in all areas of education. Through Educolor, I have not only been encouraged to be more active in making sure that teachers and students of color are heard but also in being a visible presence in my field while encouraging the same of others. I would not have made it through my first year in educational technology without this important group of people. I would not have continued to speak up at my job, in my state, or globally because my frustrations were that it seemed that issues concerning our needs were mute. They seemed to be anyway.

Jovan Miles, an educator from Atlanta, Georgia, wrote a blog post in which he questioned the absence of black educators on Twitter. In the post, Jovan talked about his experience in participating in various chats and how there is a distinct difference in participation between chats that are more culturally specific like #blackedu and #hiphoped and chats that are educationally generic like #edchat.

Before becoming acclimated with more culturally relevant chats, I too had wondered just as much as Jovan, especially as published data states that the number of black and minority users more than double that of others. What I've come to realize is that people of color talk about what matters to them just as much as every other group. We are not present in more mainstream chats because the conversations that speak to the needs of our own professional growth as well as that of our children are not being discussed. When they are, those conversations are often too dominated by those speaking from a place of privilege without seeking real understanding.

When the privilege is dominating discussions so loudly that the needs of our kids are not heard, why should the Twitter silos that we are most comfortable with dissipate so that our voices are drowned even further?

With that said, I do believe that we need more teachers of color participating in those conversations because, whether we like it or not, mainstream Twitter conversations are changing our class-rooms. The days of a buzzword being just a phase are all but gone with social sharing and blogging. Everybody wants to flip, blend, and gamify, which are not bad ideas as long as we are considering the needs of all learners in the process. We talk about devices as if access is granted to all and individual cultures are not accustomed to their own beliefs in terms of access at home.

While Twitter is an open platform where participation can be had by all, transitioning from more culturally specific conversations to mainstream ones can be intimidating because we still very much operate in our own social circles, and when we fail to acknowledge the presence or contributions of other individuals, we are in essence saying, "Hey, this is our conversation, and you don't belong." While that statement is not directly said, the implications of it can be just as clear. If we want inclusive dialogue, we have to intentionally include. We have to be open to uncomfortable discussions while also acknowledging that, through moments of discomfort, we can learn much and grow as long as we are open to doing so.

At the end of the day, what matters most is that the considerations for classrooms, when it

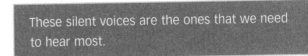

These silent voices are the ones that we need to hear most.

comes to technology, are cognizant of the needs of more than just the kids with devices, access, and privilege but kids who are typically on the side of equity that have yet to garner their own hashtag.

CHAPTER 5 REFLECTIONS

1. How are you making sure to extend technology training or leadership roles to teachers of color?
2. What can you do to intentionally make sure that teachers of color are extended professional learning opportunities?
3. What will be your plan of action to include the input of diverse teachers when addressing needs of diverse learners?

A Personal Reflection on Missing Voices

When I agreed to write this book, it was tough to differentiate among my personal experiences as a teacher, woman, and person of color. I found that what I thought to be the case wasn't really the case, and this part of the process bothered me greatly. For example, I wanted to write about the barriers that hold women back, yet I am in a district surrounded by women in leadership. I wanted to write about the lack of opportunity given to teachers of color, yet depending on where I turned, I saw opportunity there. Then it dawned on me that where I was looking was in the areas of curriculum and campus leadership, not technology. There is a difference, although there should not be.

I am fortunate in that I am in a personal space where I can freely say what needs to be said regardless of who is listening. I must acknowledge that I would not be as comfortable as I am had it not been for my being connected to people like Jose Vilson, Sabrina Stevens, Melinda Anderson, Audrey Watters, Chris Lehmann, Diana Laufenberg, or Xian Barrett. Through them, I learned the power of an open door. Open doors lead to room for conversation. Conversations must then lead to action. Through this process, I own that my action is to make sure that the voices of teachers, students, women, and people of color are no longer silent whispers in the back of the room but heard loud and clear among the chatter that inhabits our space.

Additional Resources

EdTechWomen. (n.d.). About. Retrieved March 4, 2014, from http://edtech women.com/

National Center for Women & Information Technology. (n.d.). Retrieved June 10, 2014, from http://www.nc wit.org/

Sinek, S. (2009). *Start with why: How great leaders inspire everyone to take action.* New York: Portfolio.

Vilson, J. L. (2014). *This is not a test: A new narrative on race, class, and education.* Chicago, IL: Haymarket Books.

A SAGE Company

Corwin is committed to improving education for all learners by publishing books and other professional development resources for those serving the field of PreK–12 education. By providing practical, hands-on materials, Corwin continues to carry out the promise of its motto: **"Helping Educators Do Their Work Better."**